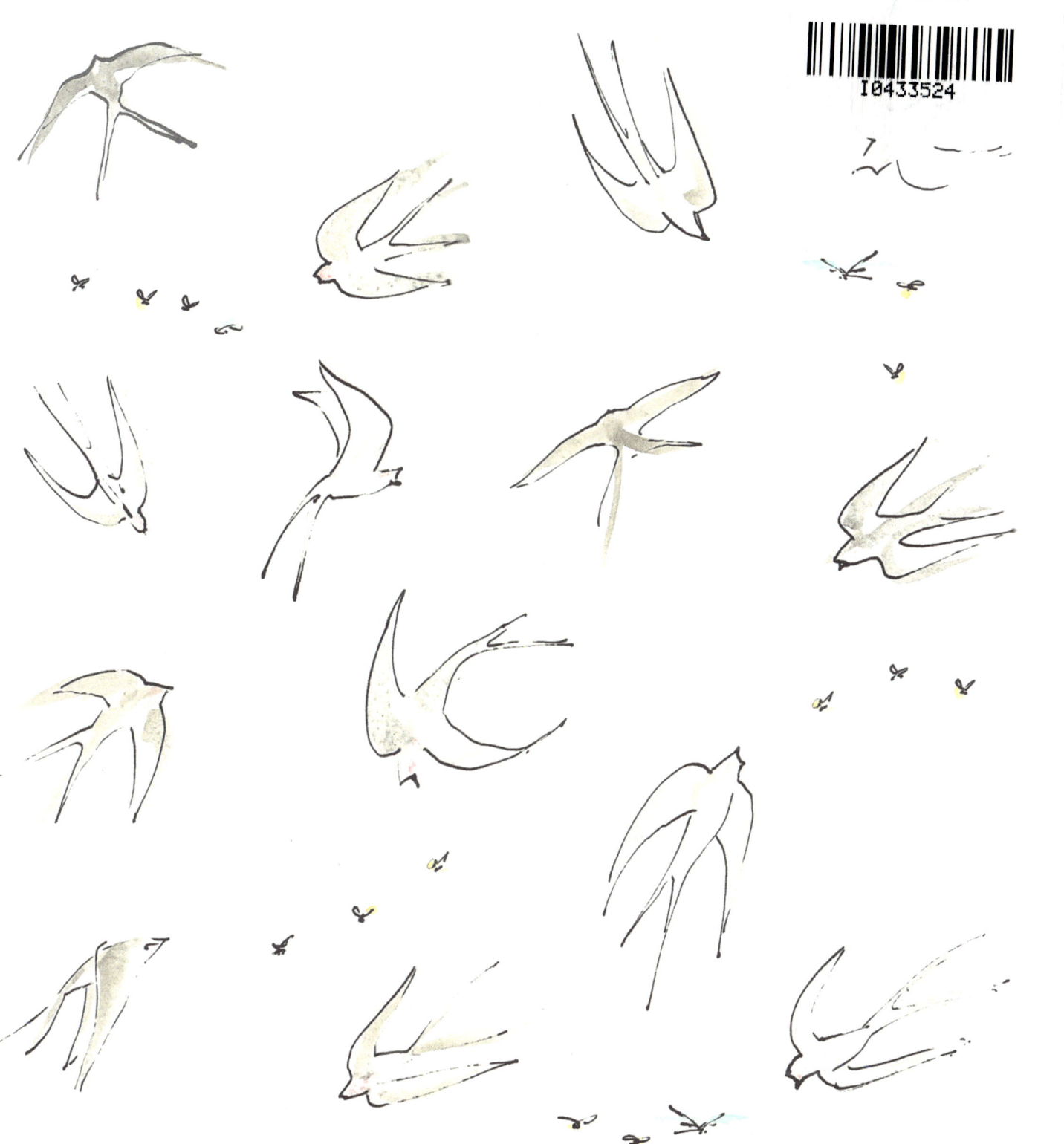

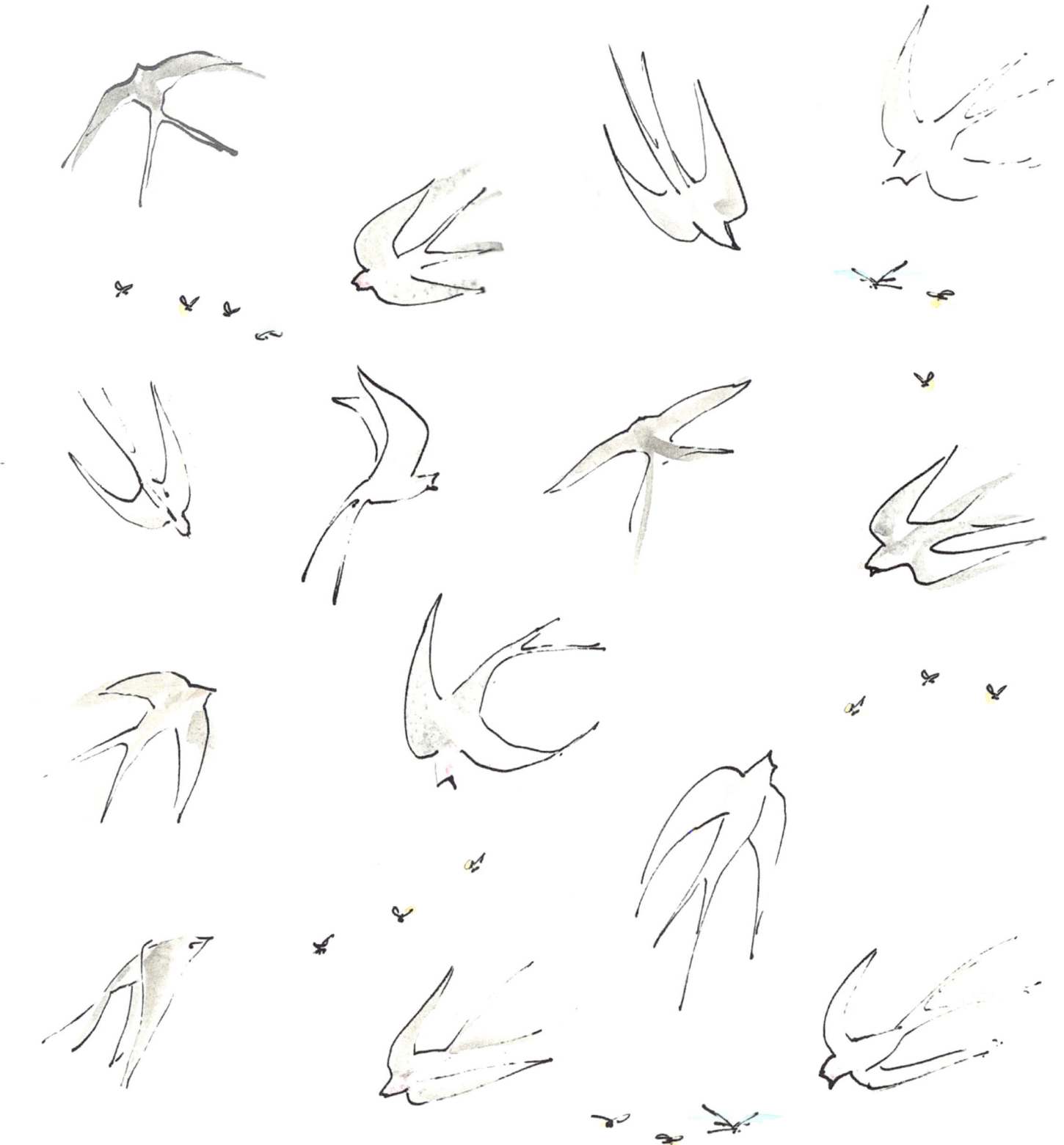

Where Do the Swallows Go?

A Visual Journey

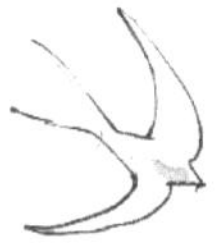

Cassie Herschel-Shorland

My Fat Fox Ltd

MMXIV

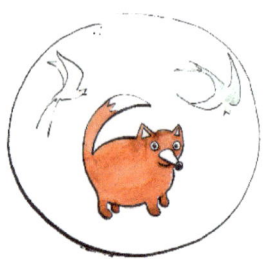

My Fat Fox Ltd
86 Gladys Dimson House
London E7 9DF
United Kingdom

www.myfatfox.co.uk

All rights reserved. No part of this publication may be used, reproduced, re-sold, lent, hired out, circulated or transmitted in any manner whatsoever, electronic or mechanical, in any form of binding or cover other than that in which it is published and without a similar condition including this condition being imposed on the subsequent purchaser without written permission from the author, except in the case of brief quotations embodied in articles or reviews.

Where Do the Swallows Go © 2014 Cassie Herschel-Shorland

The rights of Cassie Herschel-Shorland to be identified as the author and illustrator of this work have been asserted by her in accordance with the Copyright, Designs and Patents Act, 1988

Cover design
© 2014 Cassie Herschel-Shorland

ISBN 978-1-905747-40-5

This book is for Sam

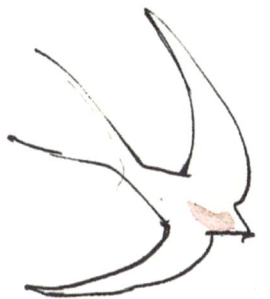

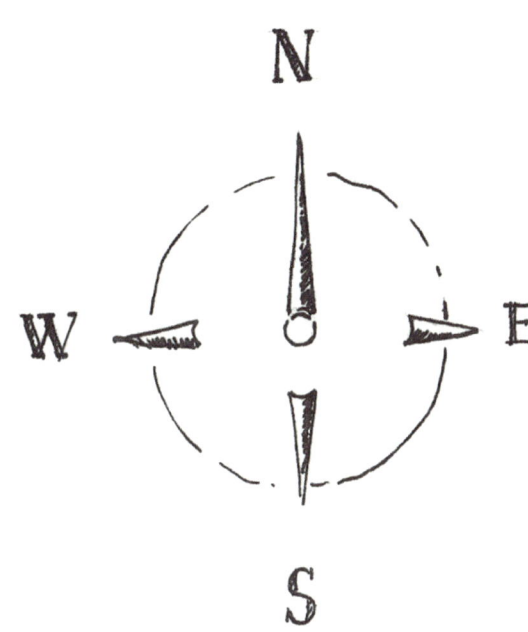

With thanks to David
for the natural history accuracy

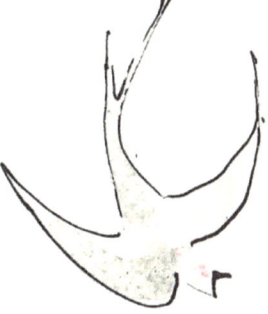

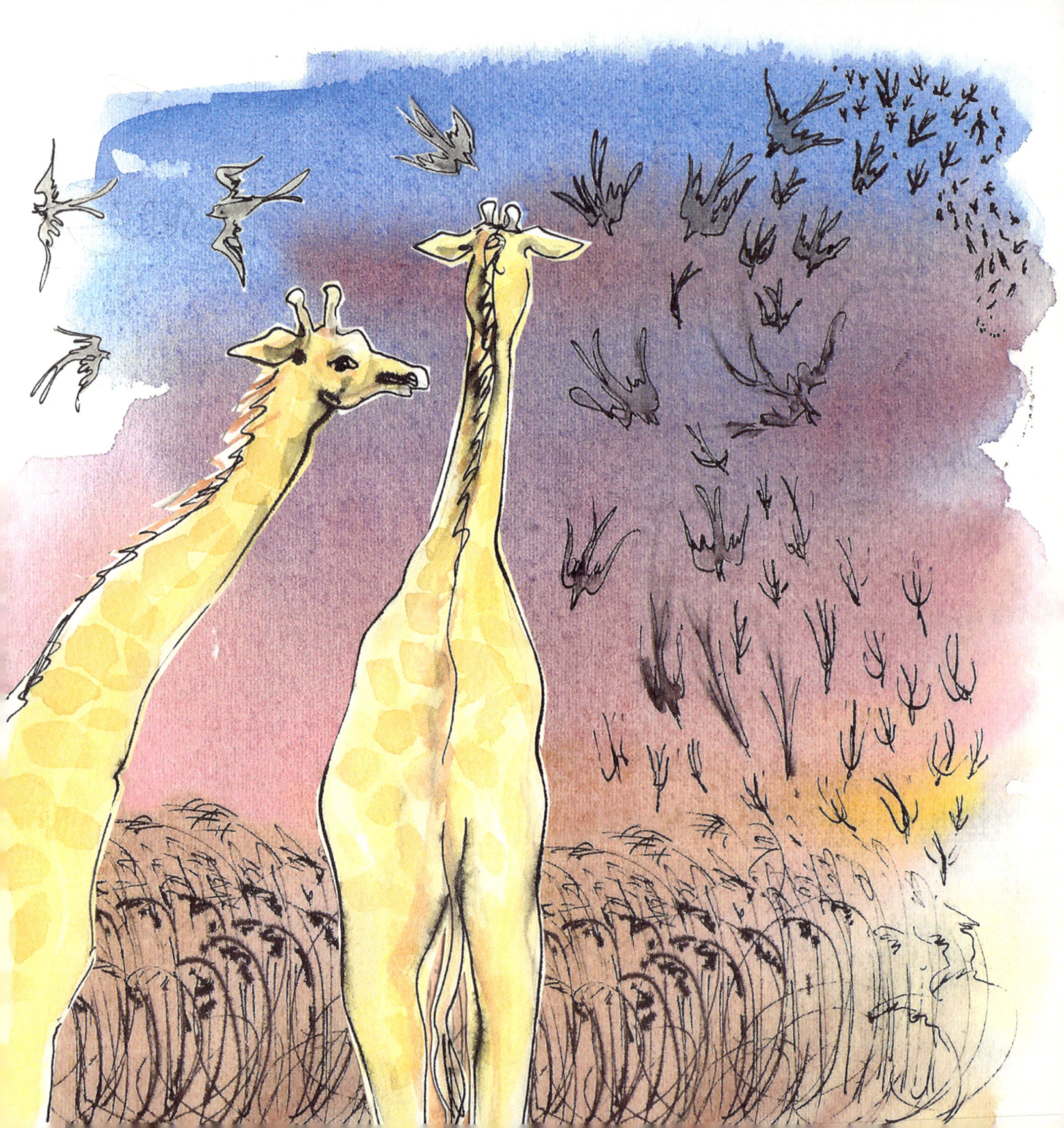

Where are all the swallows?

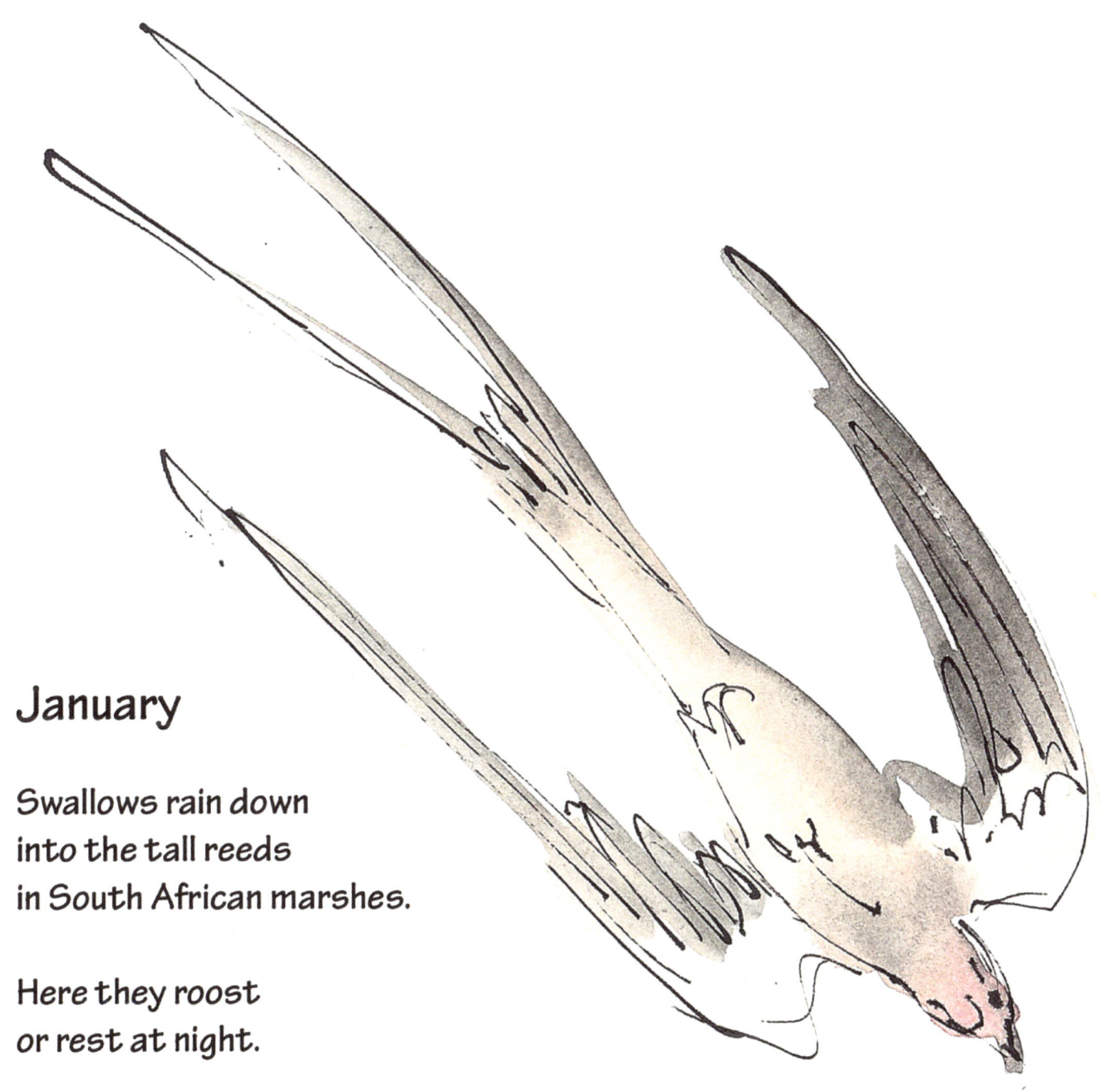

January

Swallows rain down
into the tall reeds
in South African marshes.

Here they roost
or rest at night.

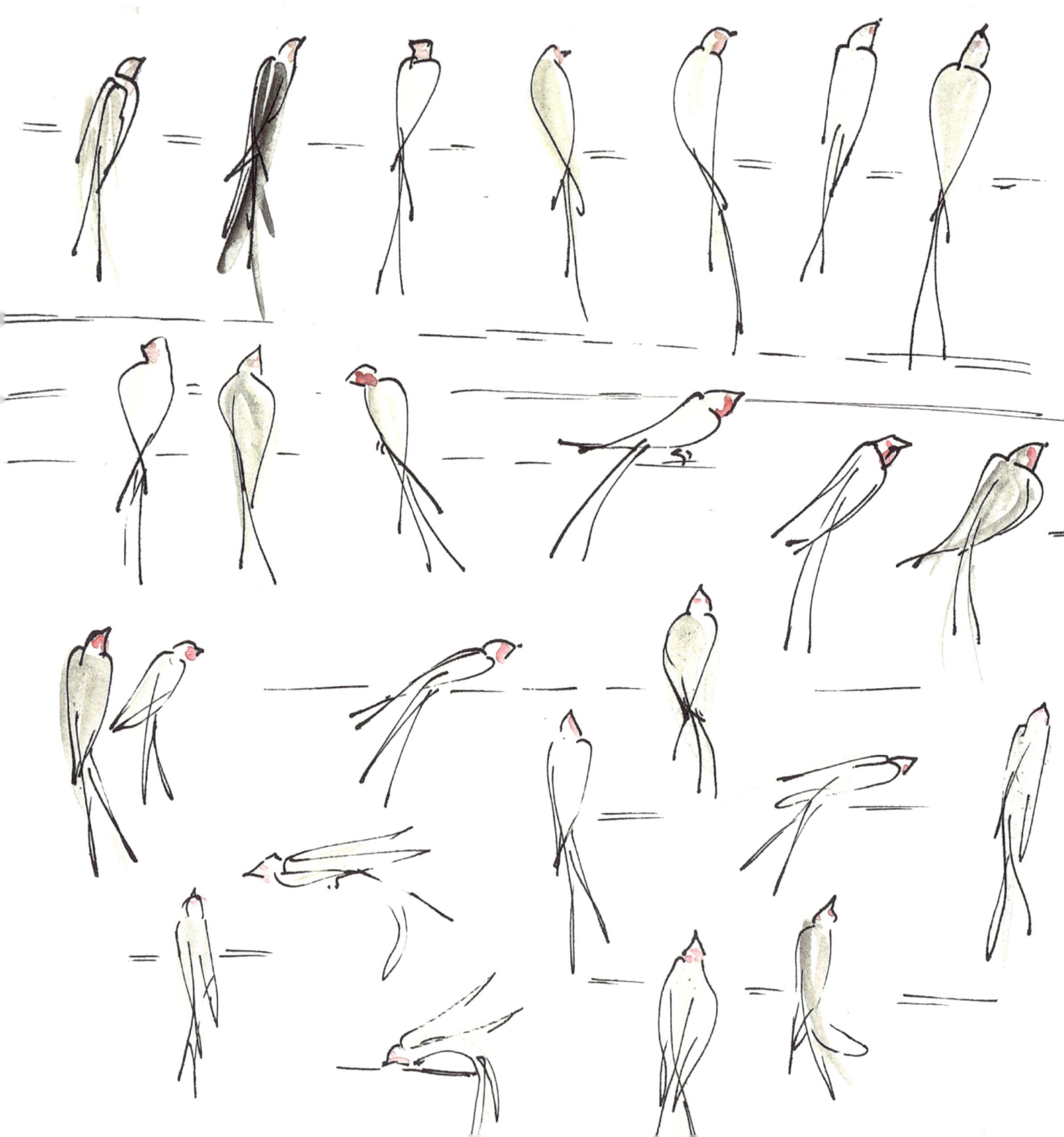

Why do swallows 'hang out' on wires?

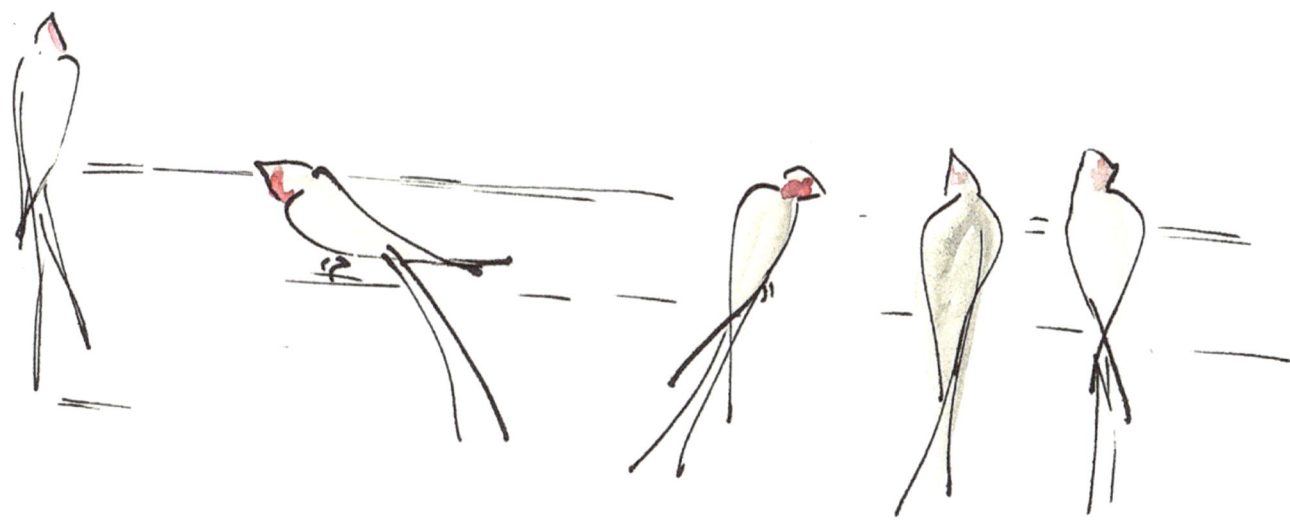

February

Rows and rows of swallows gather on telegraph wires ready to return to where they were born.

They will breed and have their family in the same place.

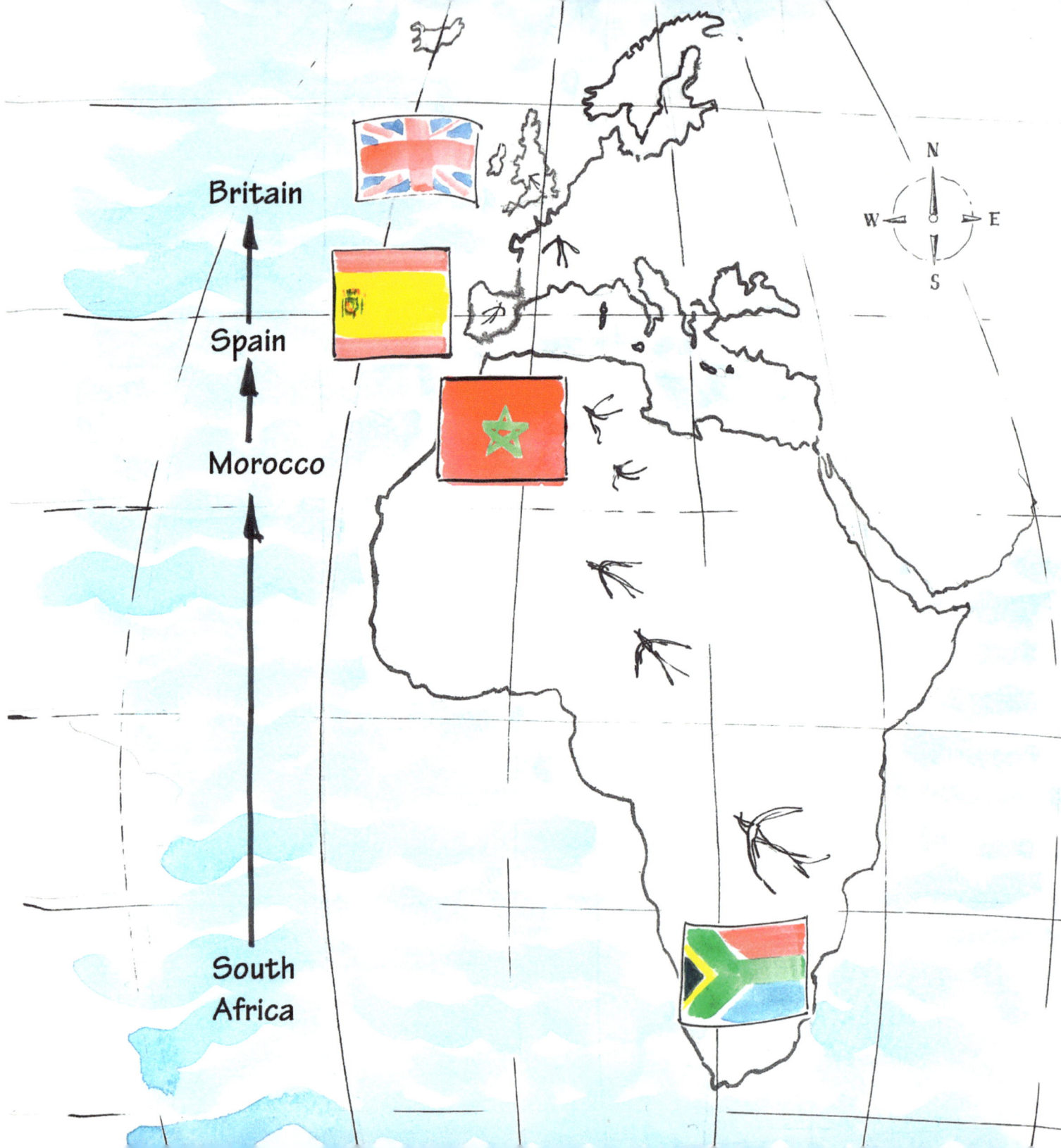

Journey facts...

March

They go north, flying at 20 miles per hour.
Each bird covers about 200 miles per day.
Swallows only fly in daylight, their whole journey is 6 to 9,000 miles!

Water, water everywhere...

April

Scooping water as they go, swallows drink on the wing.

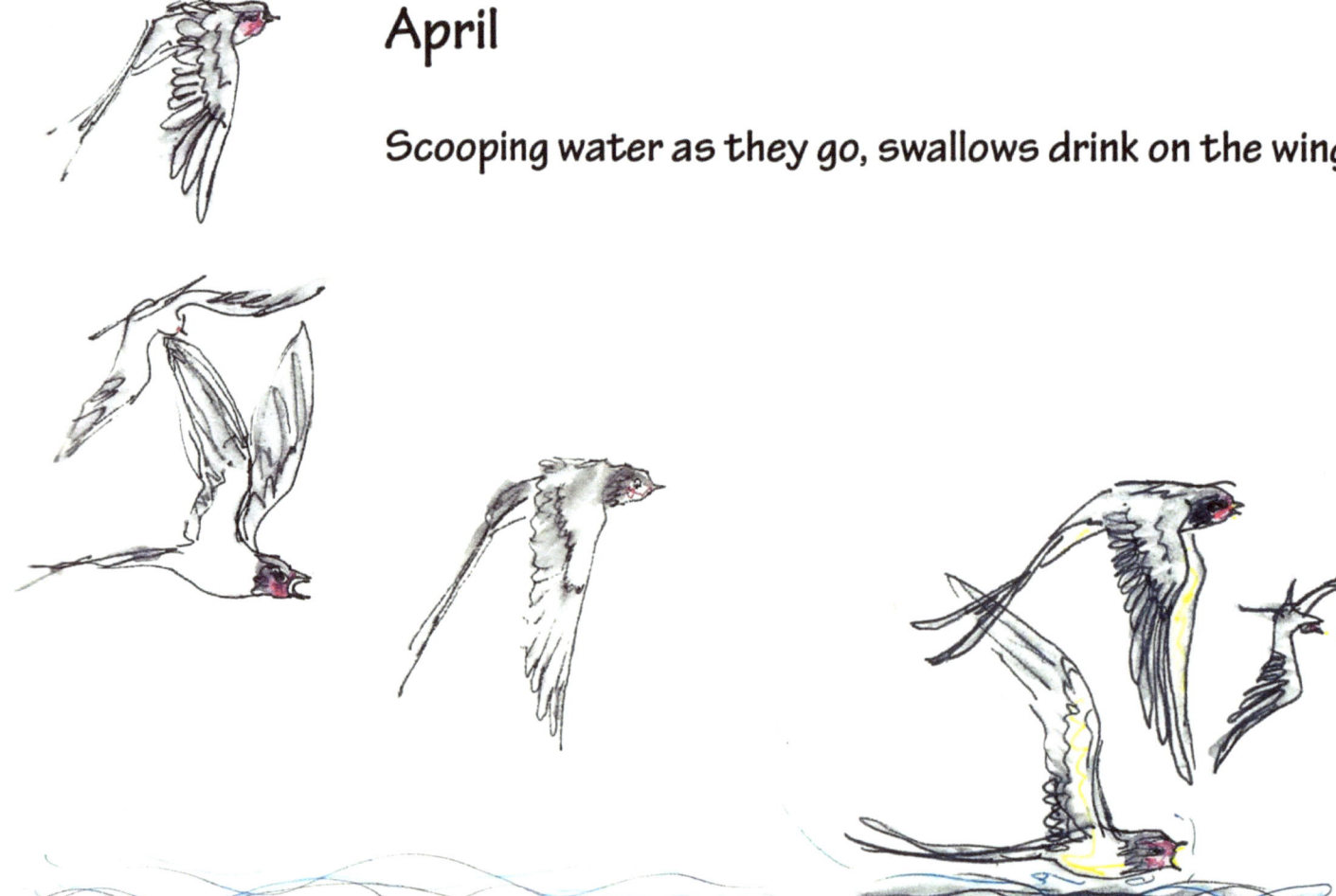

Eviction!

May

Breeding places such as barns and out-houses are threatened by big building projects.

Swallows make their nests from mud and plant fibre. A pair often rears more than one family or brood each year.

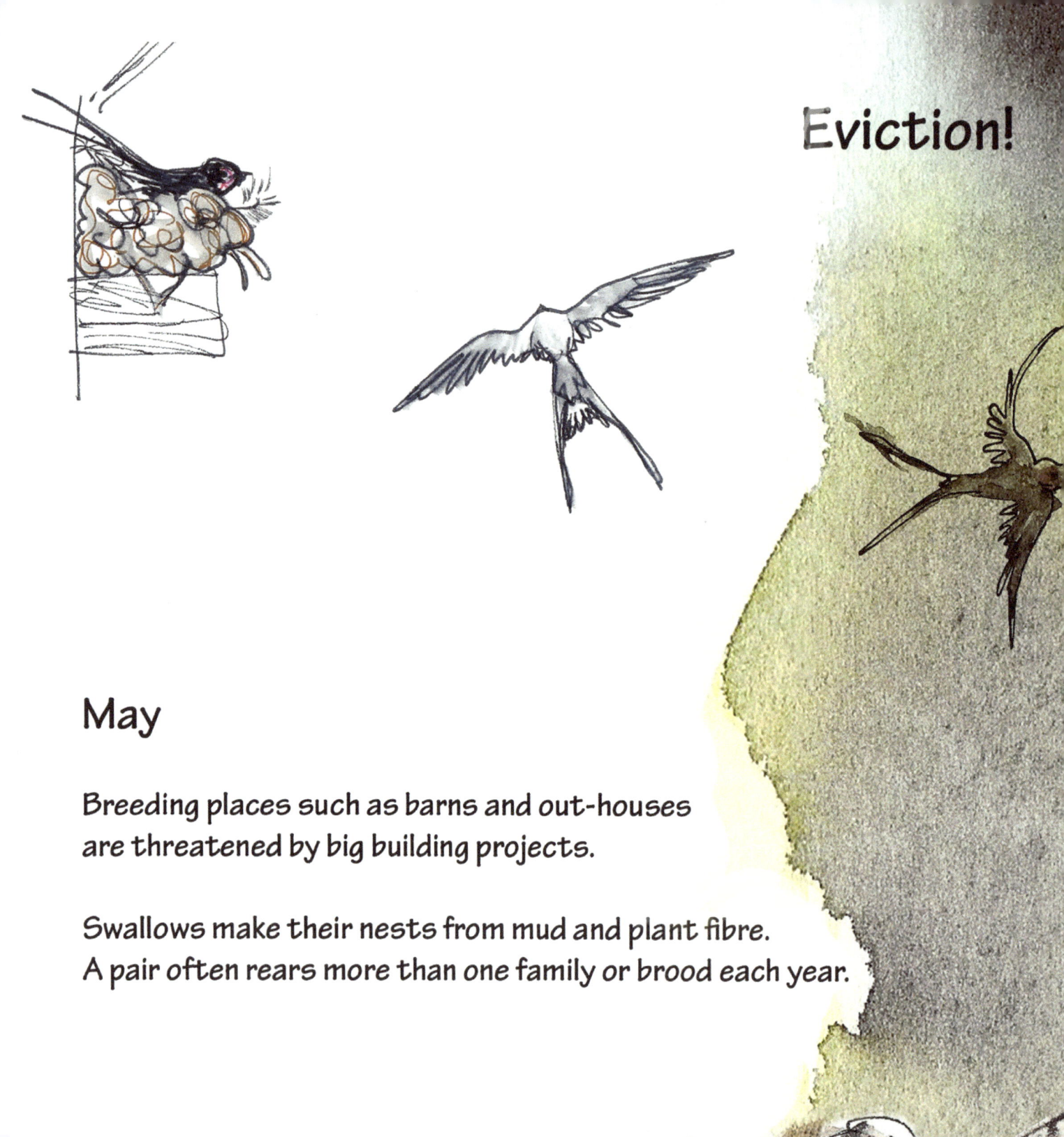

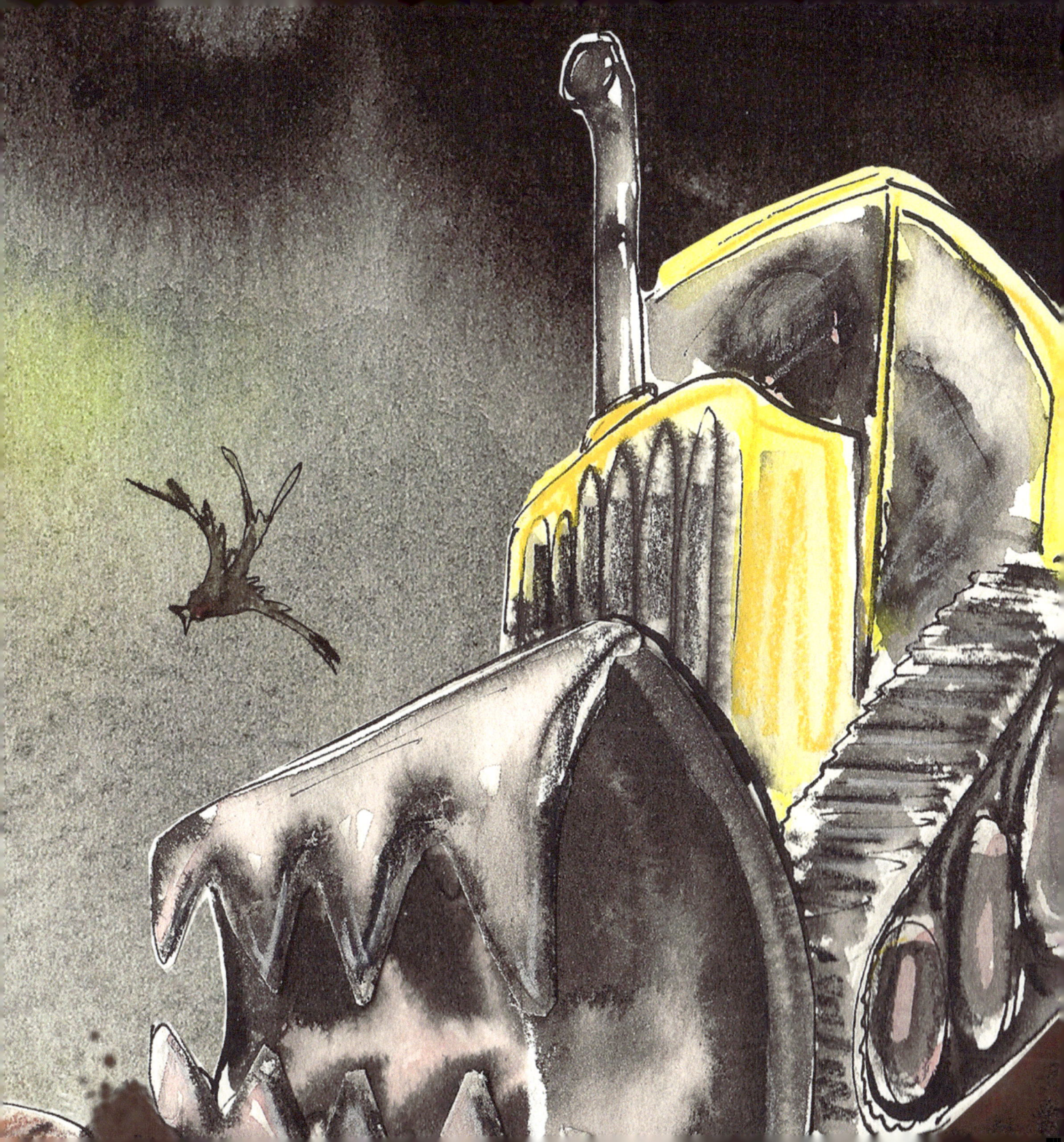

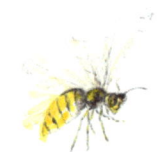
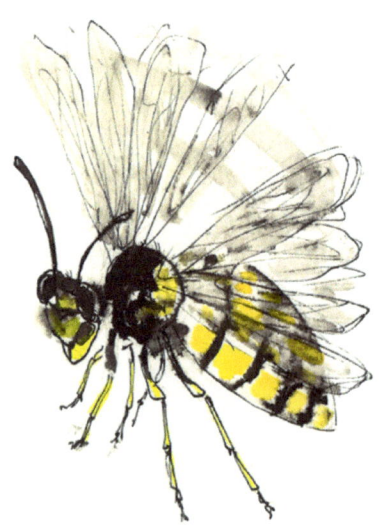

What do swallows eat?

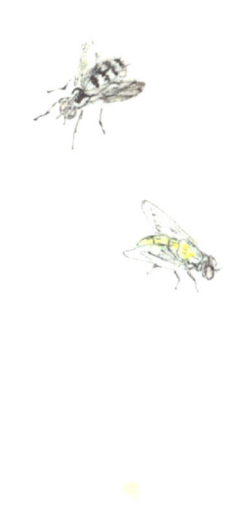

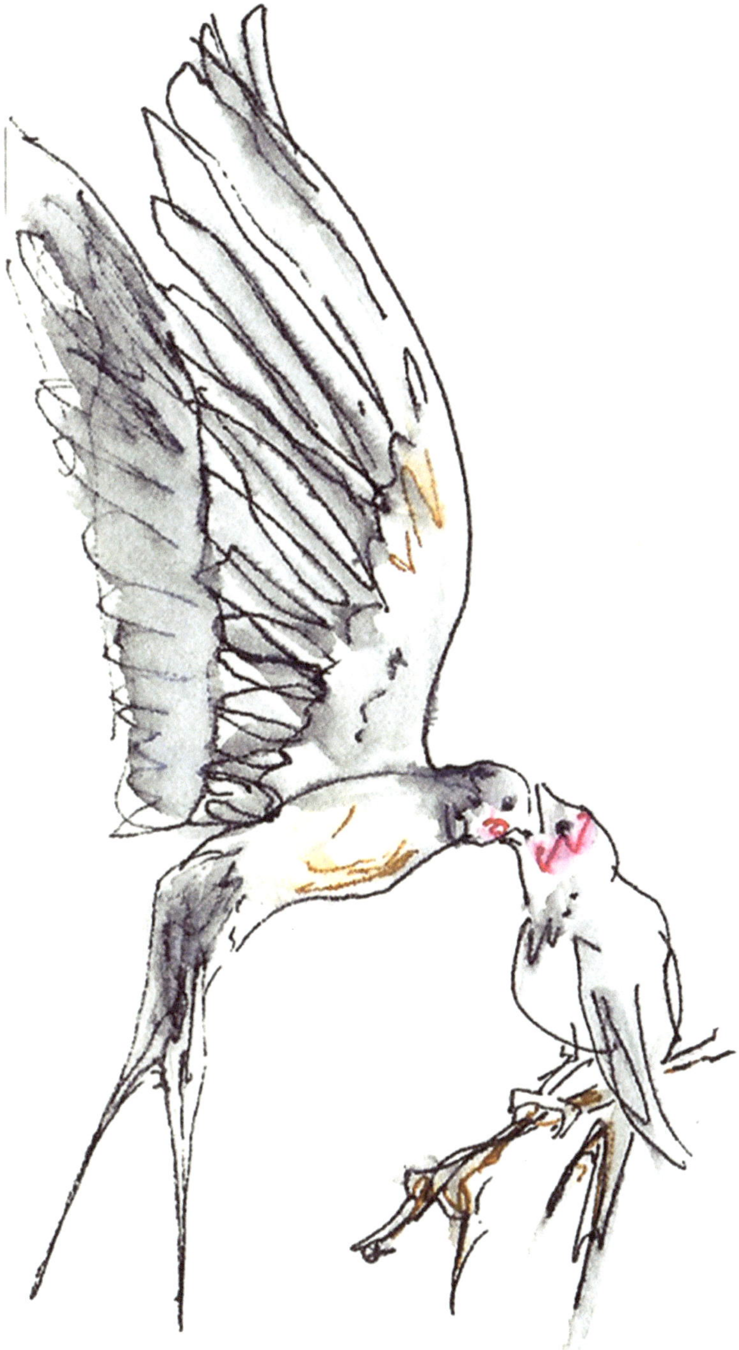

June

Swallows eat insects caught in flight.

The shape of their tails help swallows' aerodynamic moves to catch their food.

Why do swallows go?

July

At the end of Summer swallows migrate south,
as do other birds such as cuckoos and wagtails.

With a long flight ahead the birds feed and build up strength.
Is it the colder weather or an internal clock that makes them
know when to go?

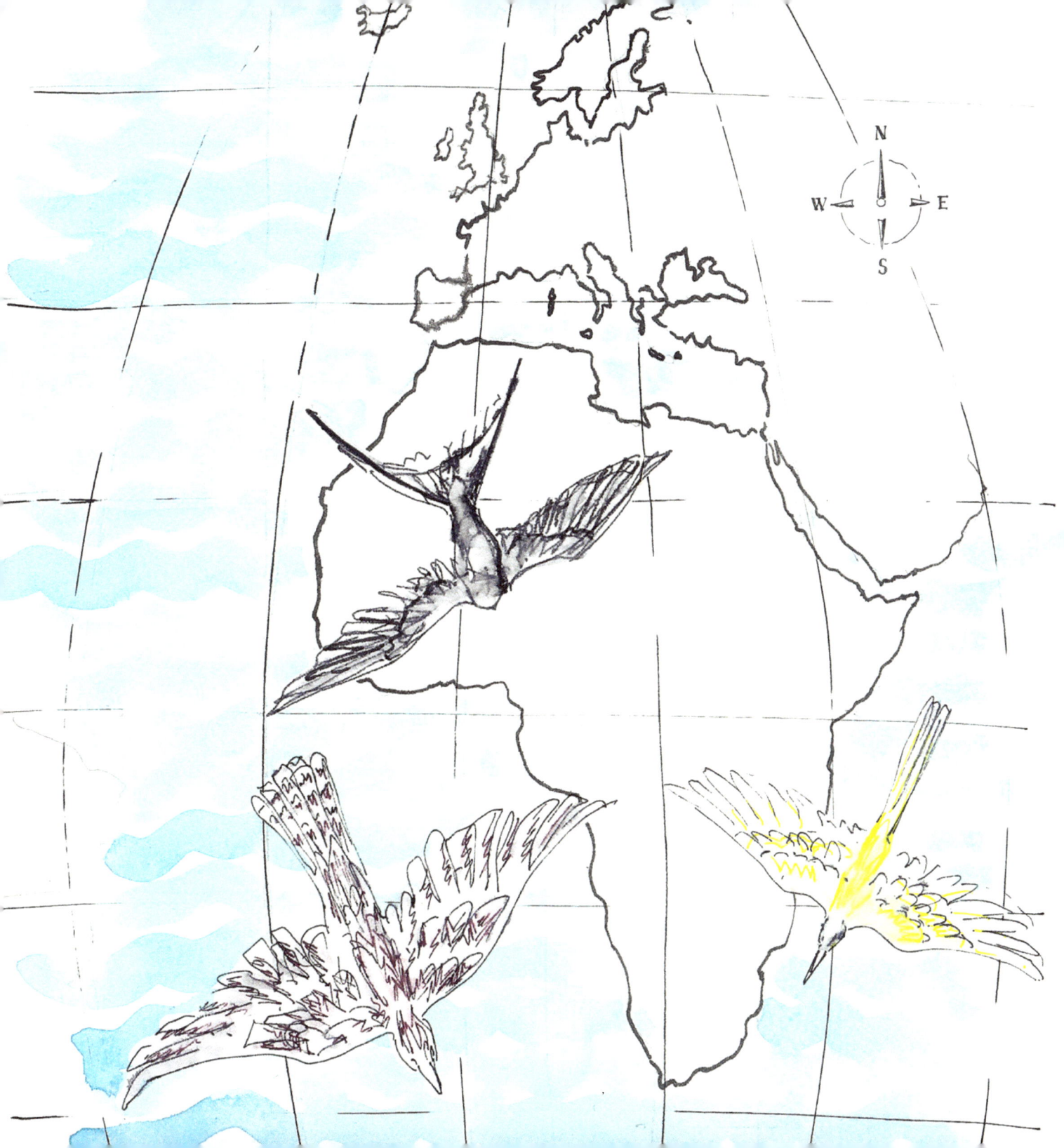

Pond dipping
August

People in England once thought swallows slept at the bottom of ponds and lakes over winter.

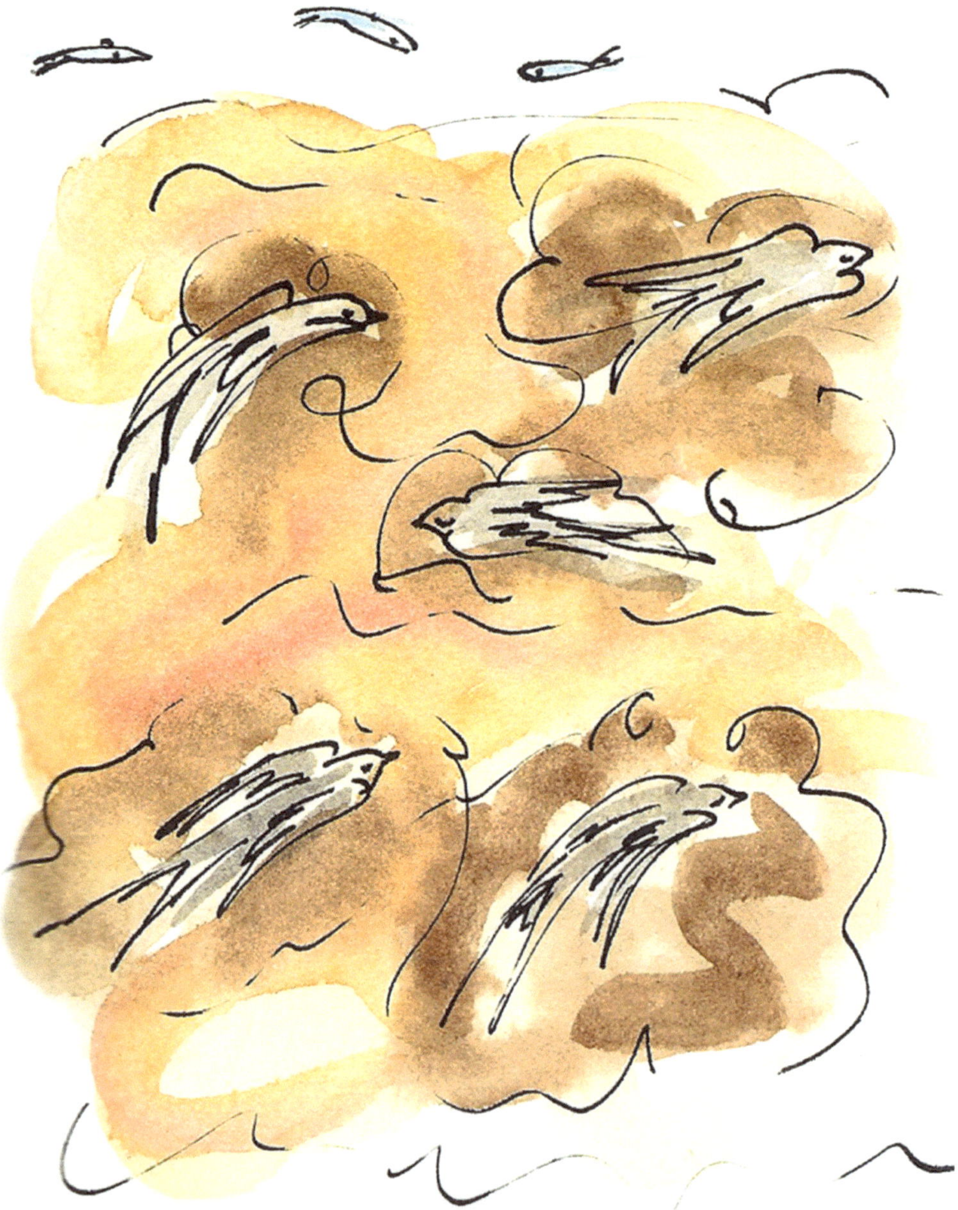

A rough ride

September

They fly across the channel, over land through France and onward above the Pyrenees. Swallows use landmarks such as mountain ranges and rivers to navigate by day.

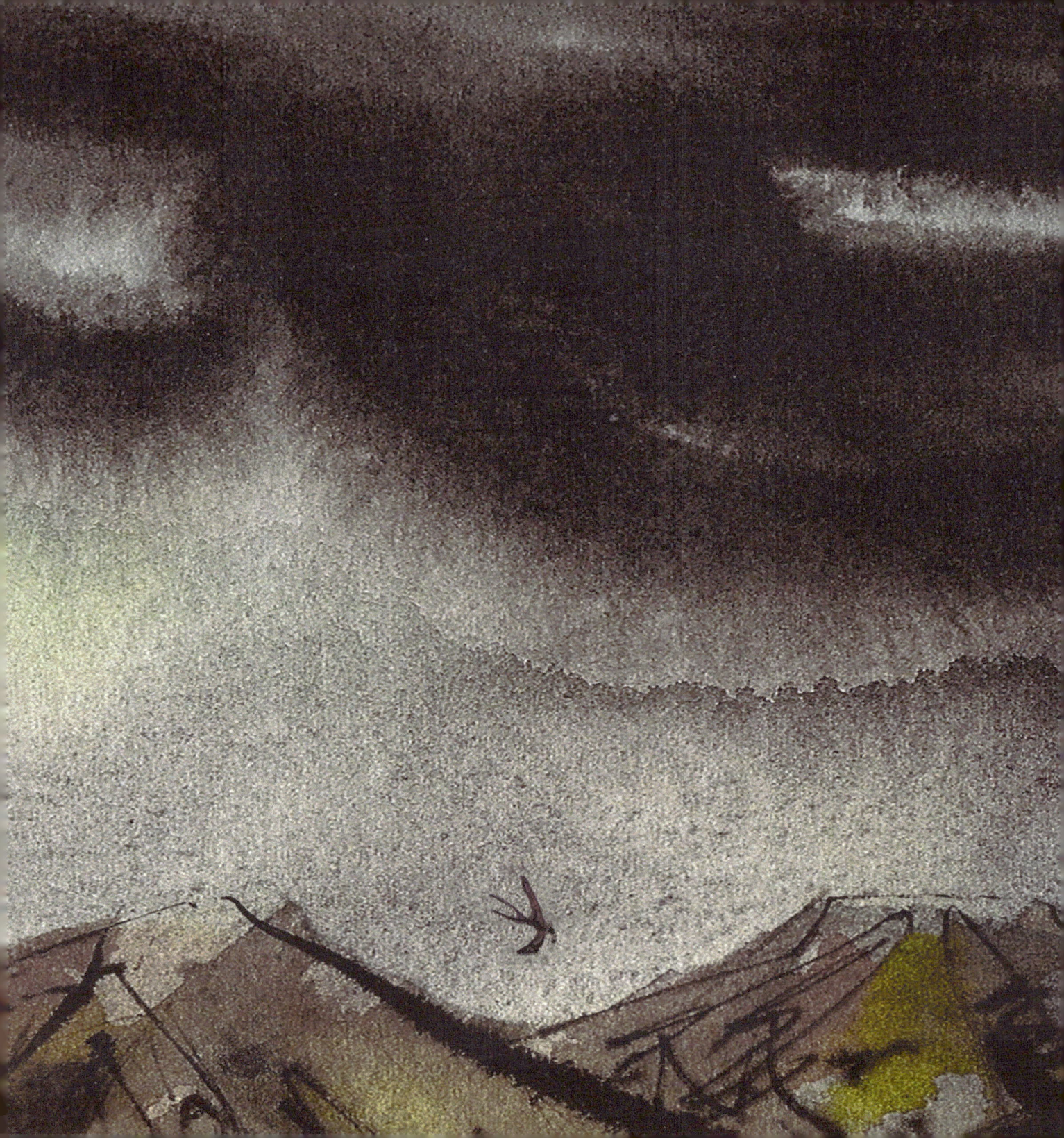

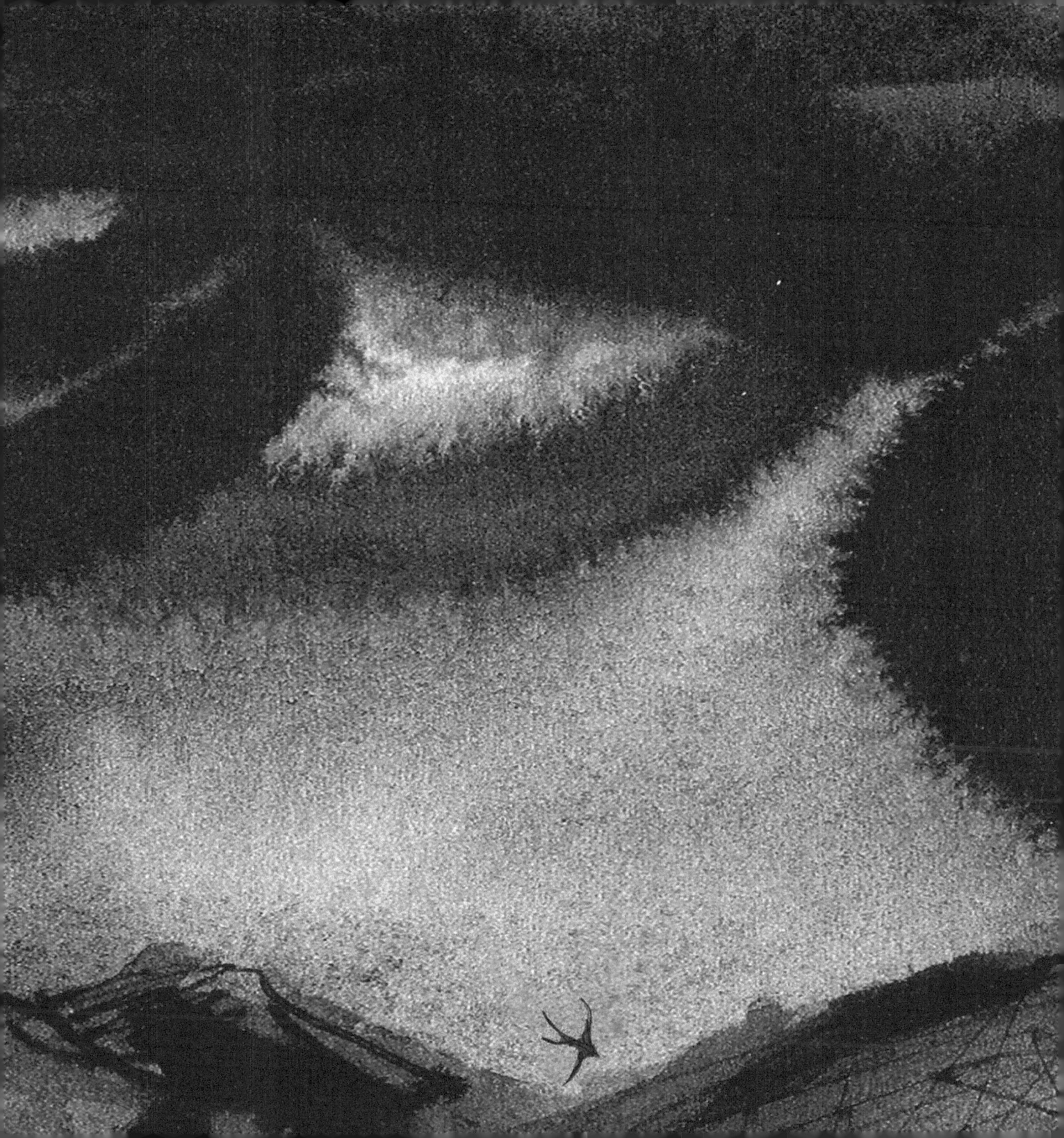

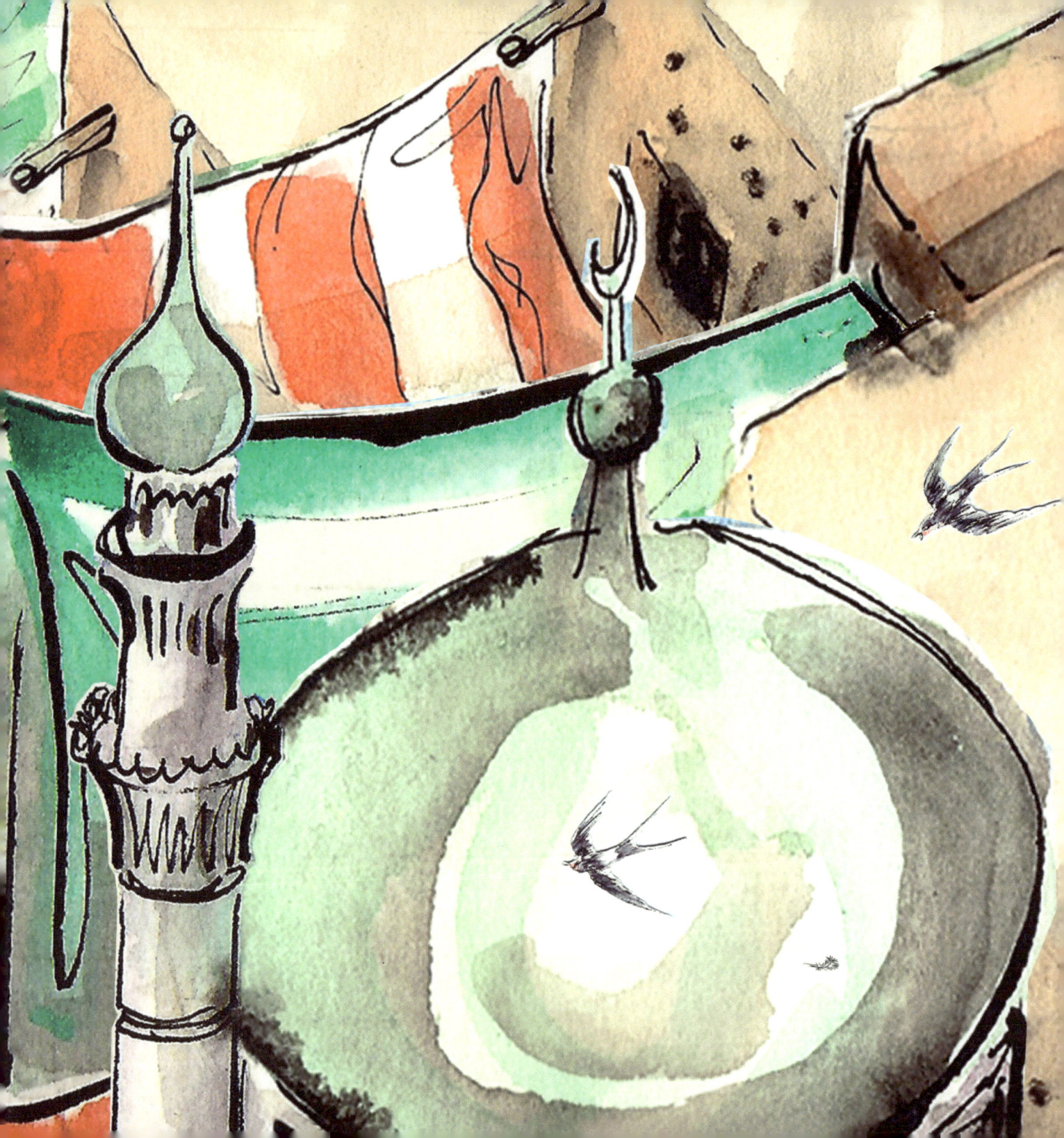

Exotic times

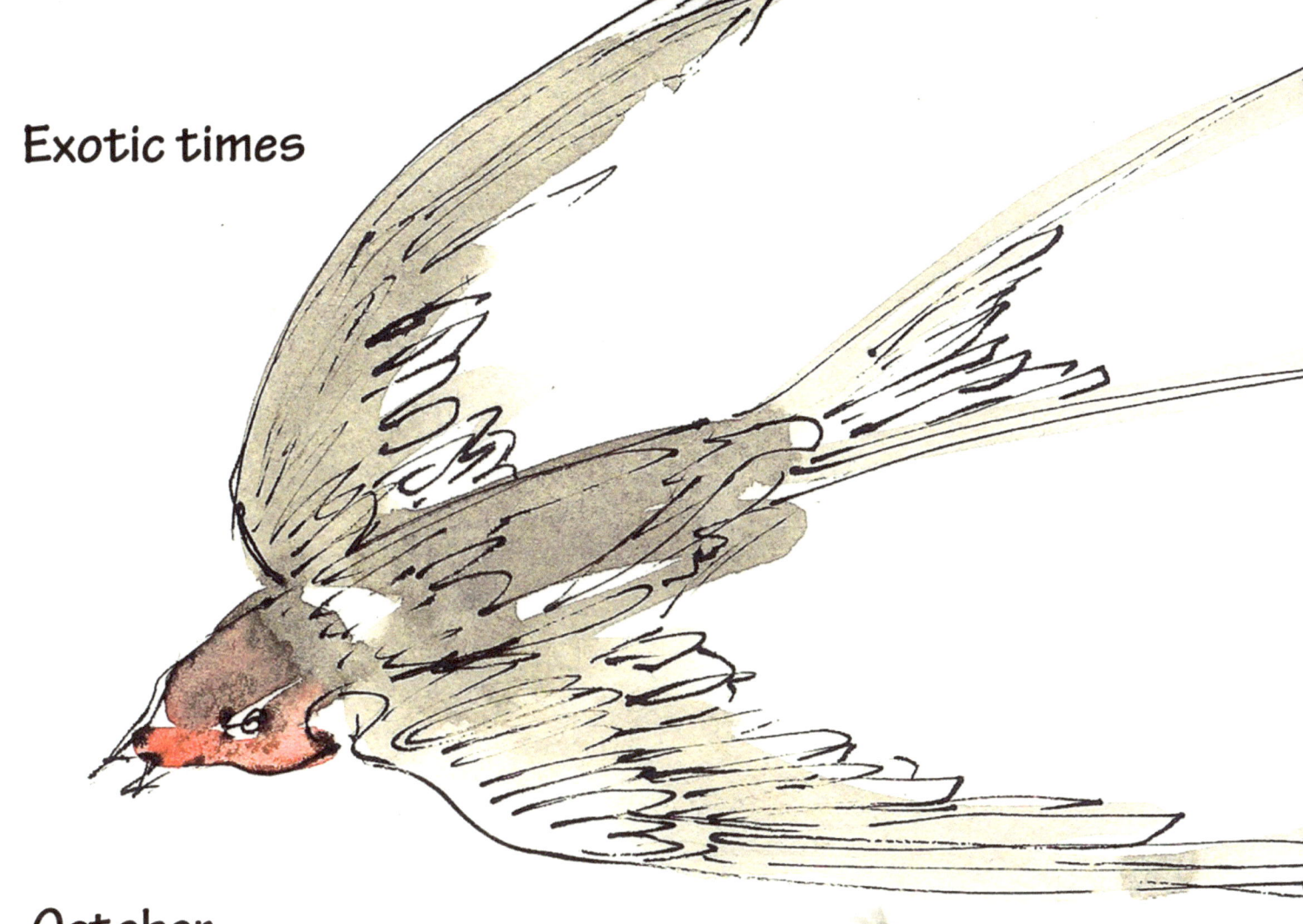

October

Colours of the birds' feathers (plumage) changes, just like putting on holiday clothes. As they travel in the brighter skies of Morocco and into North Africa their breeding plumage goes.

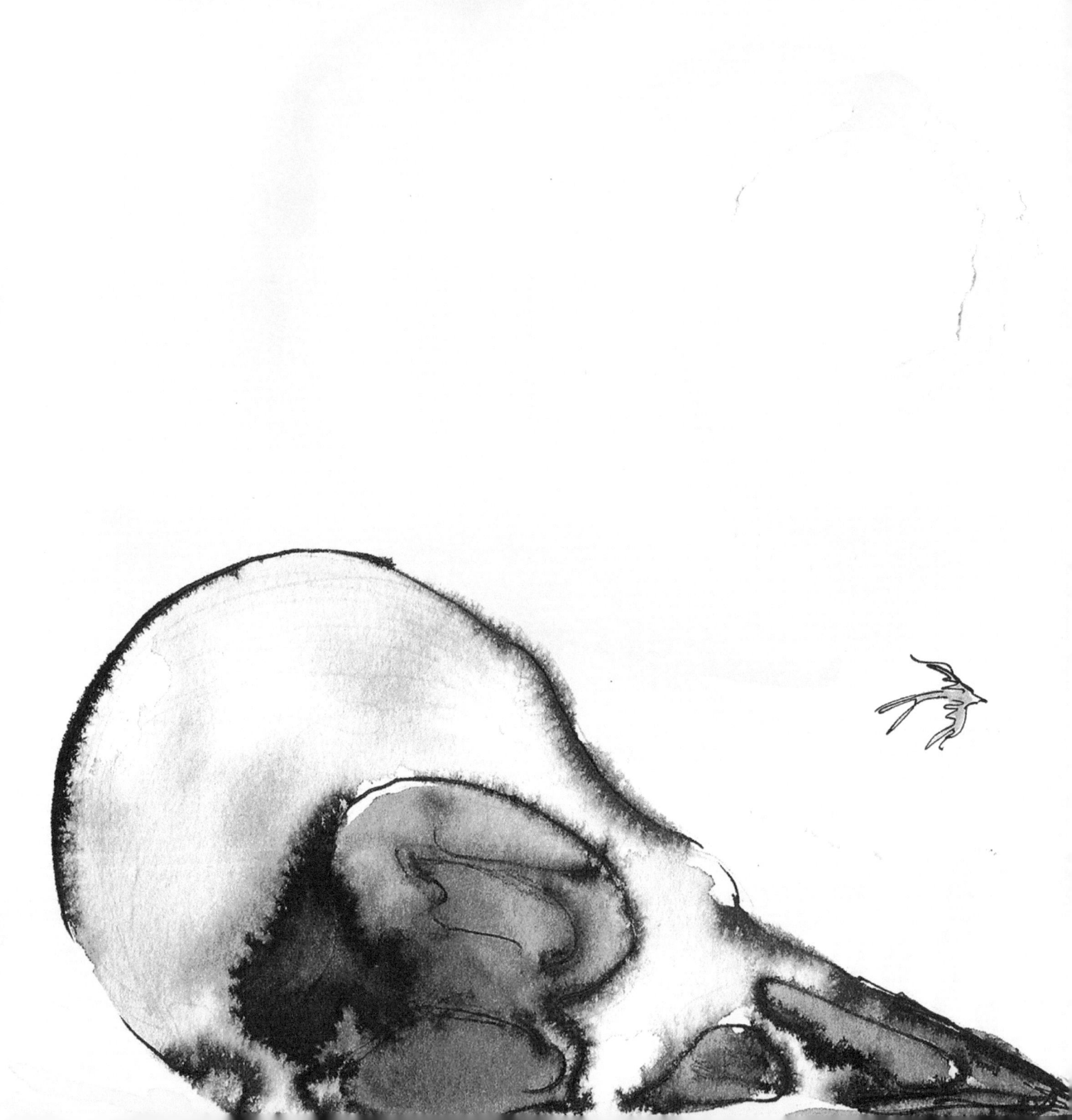

Where are all the swallows?

November

Many birds don't make it across the deserts of the Sahara.

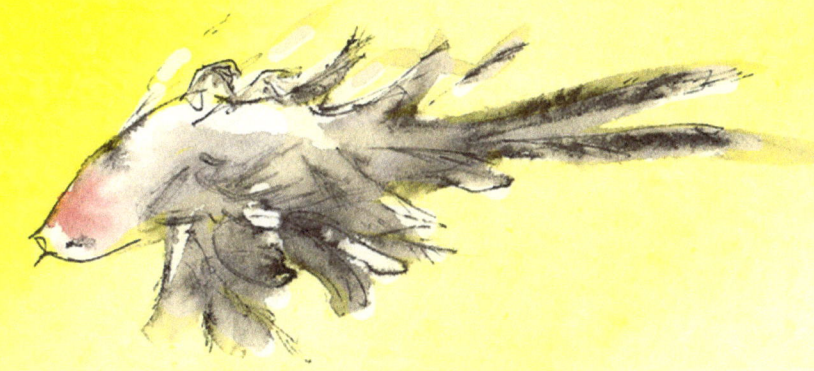

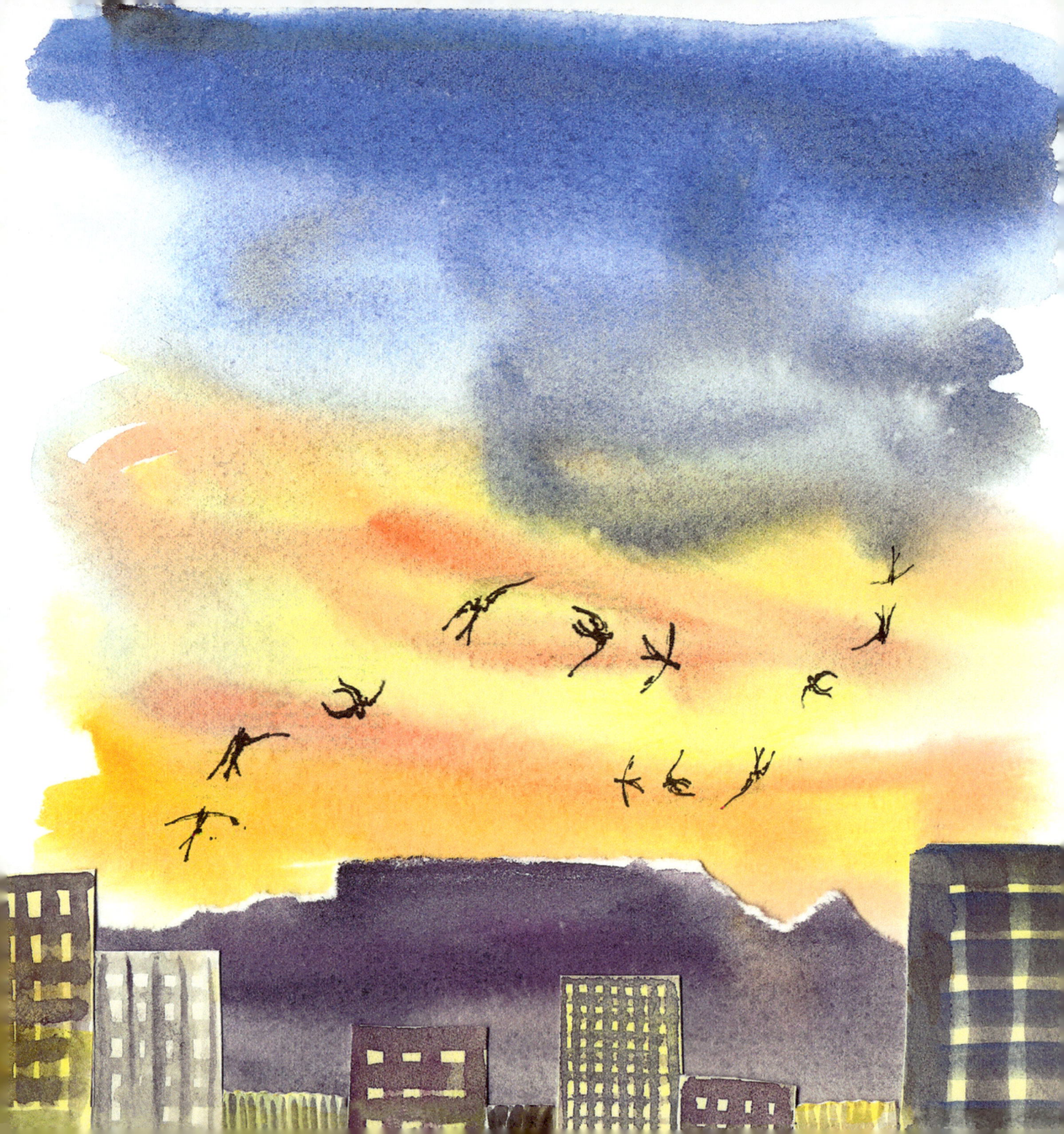

Swallows clouds

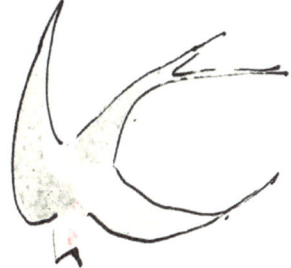

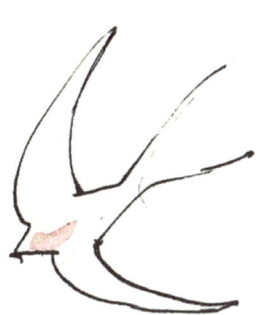
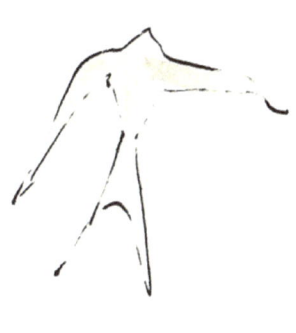

December

The strong swallows arrive back in South Africa.

Air traffic controls warn pilots if there are swallow clouds over the runways!

Journey's end...

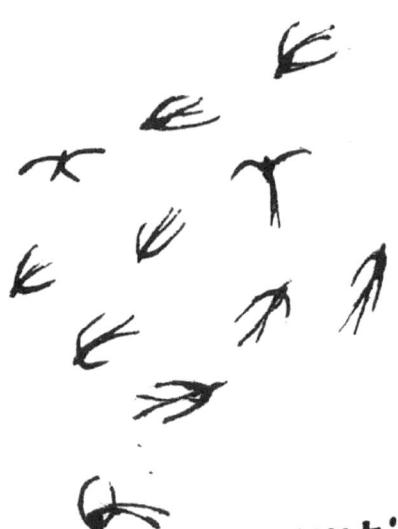

...until they fly back again next year!

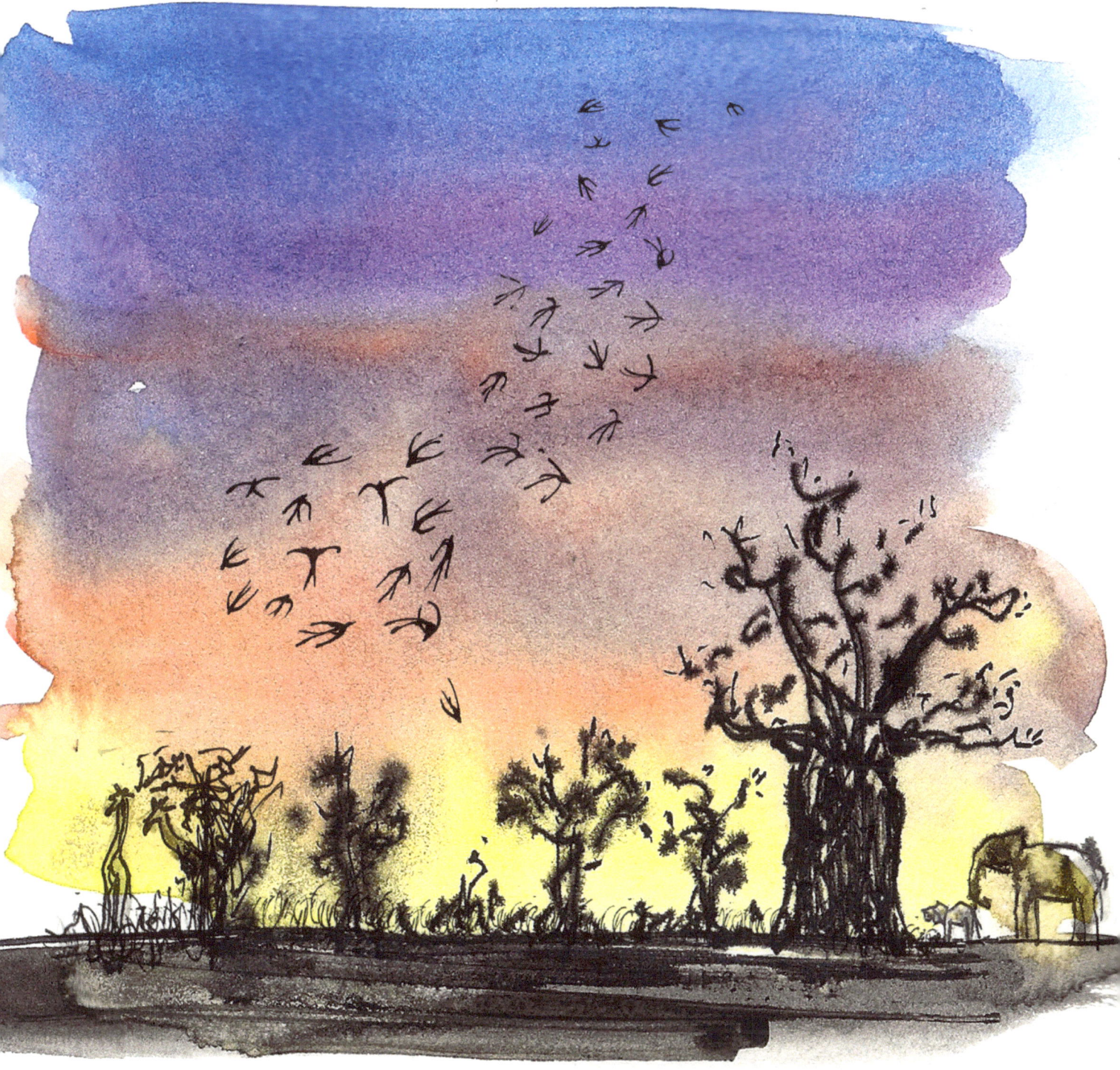

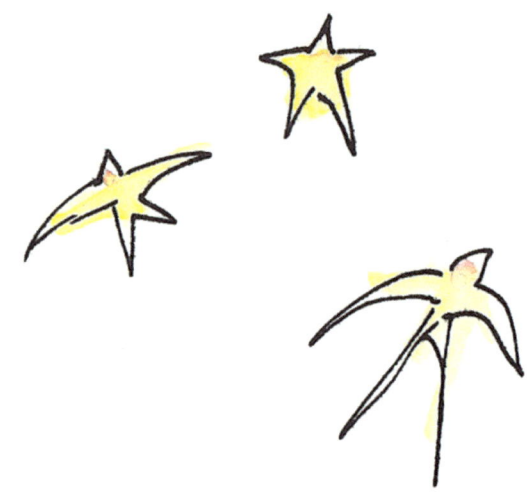

Imperishable stars

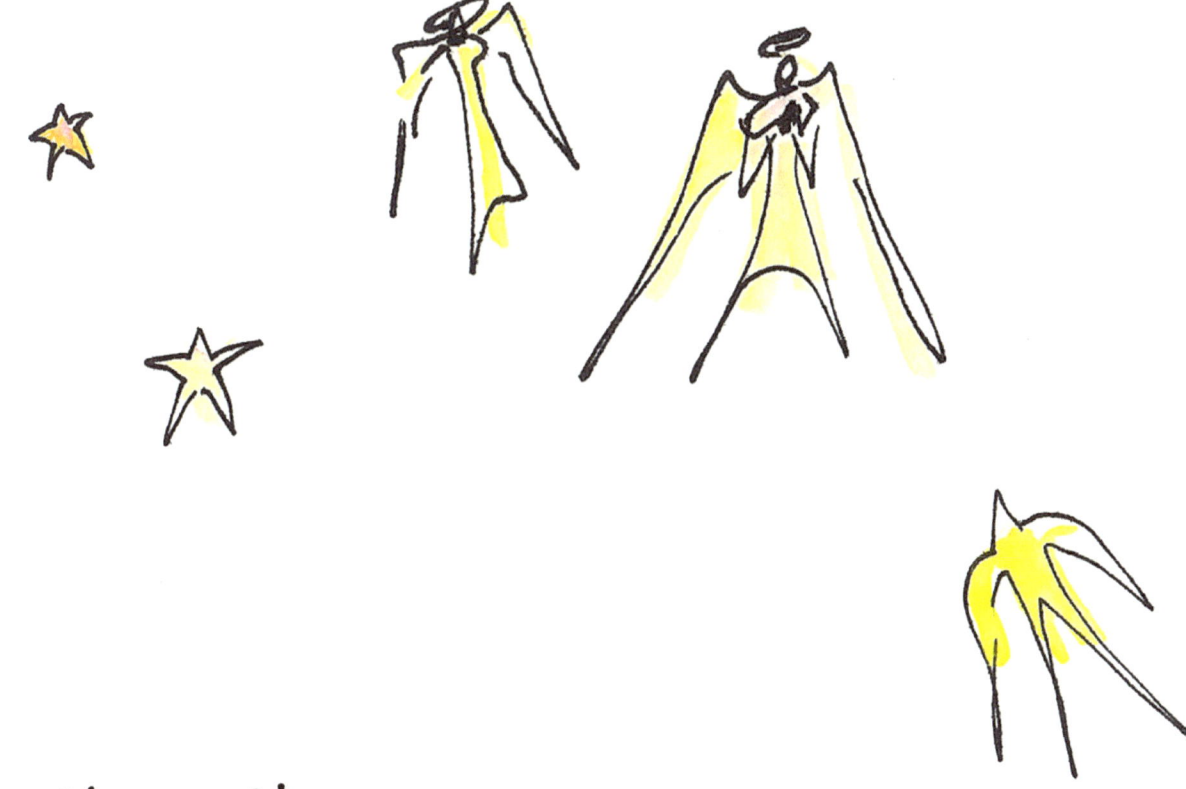

Egyptian myth

During the old kingdom swallows were associated with the stars and the souls of the dead. One pharaoh wrote: 'swallows are the imperishable stars'.

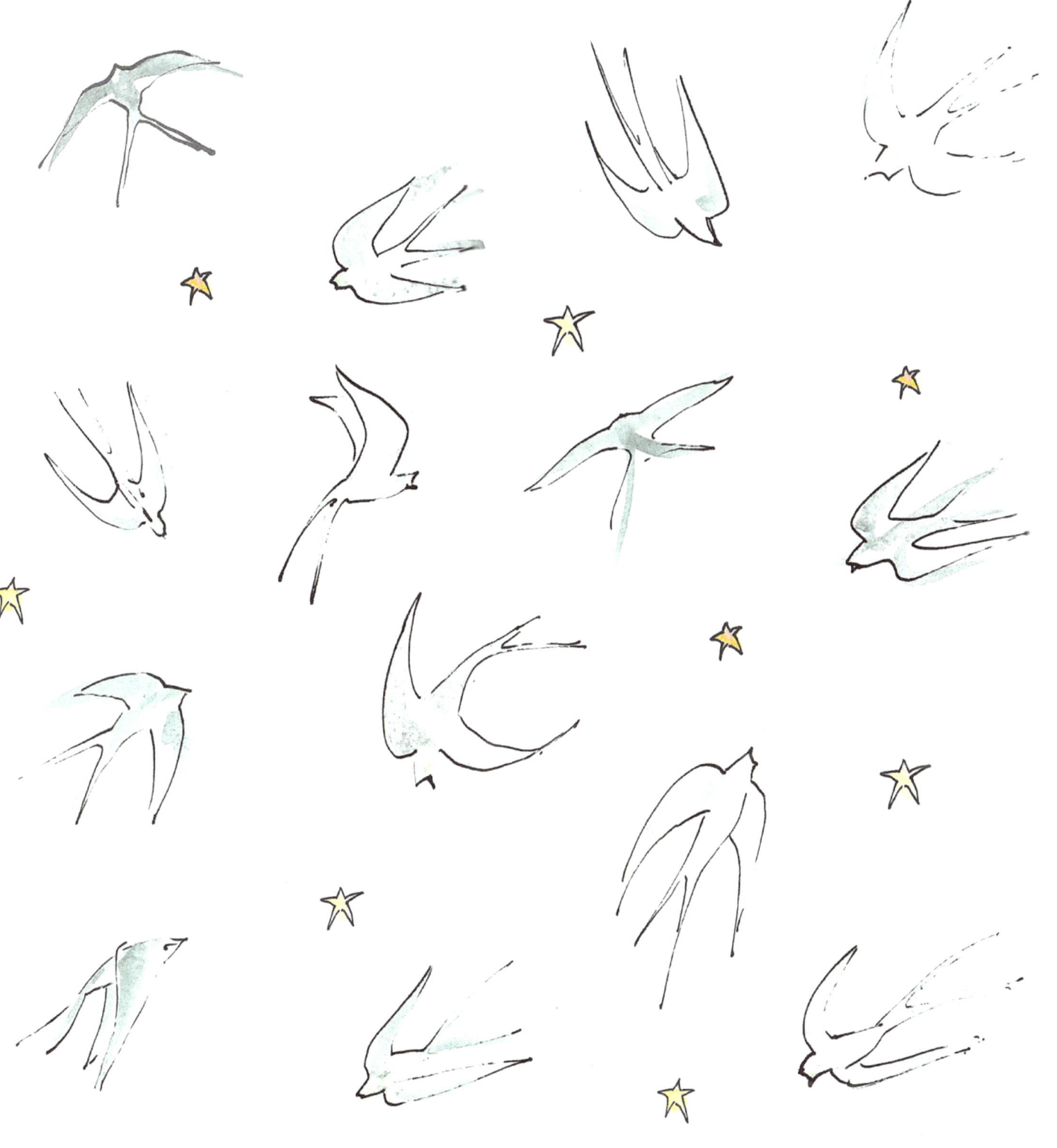

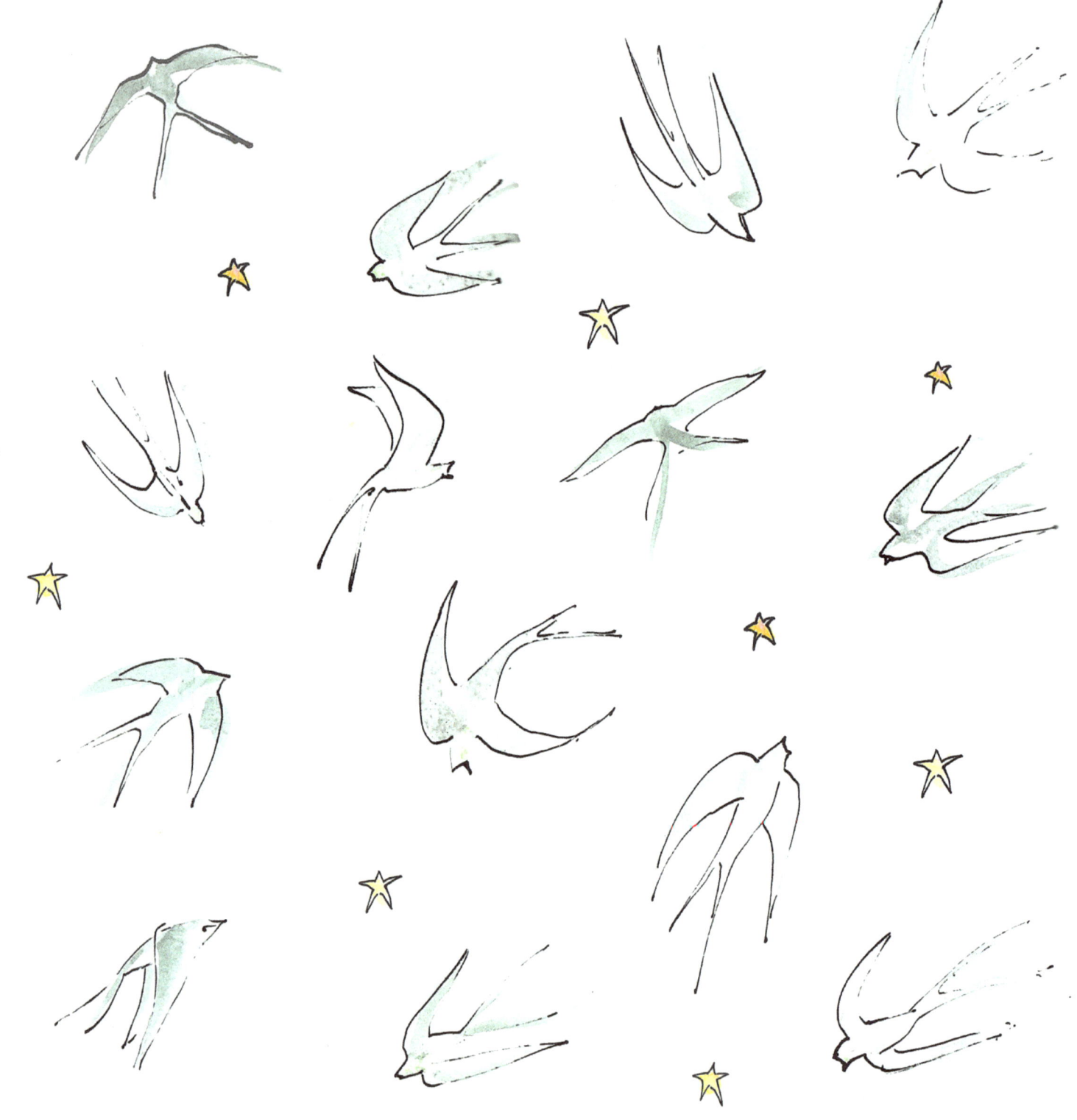

www.ingramcontent.com/pod-product-compliance
Lightning Source LLC
Chambersburg PA
CBHW040454220526
45473CB00004B/1629